# INSPIRED BY TRADITION

*Martingale*®
& COMPANY

# INSPIRED

## KAY MACKENZIE

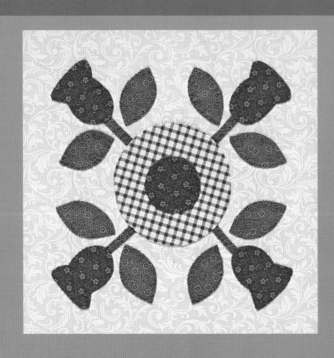

# BY TRADITION

## 50 Appliqué Blocks in 5 Sizes

Inspired by Tradition: 50 Appliqué Blocks in 5 Sizes
© 2011 by Kay Mackenzie

That Patchwork Place® is an imprint of
Martingale & Company®.

Martingale & Company
19021 120th Ave. NE, Suite 102
Bothell, WA 98011-9511
www.martingale-pub.com

## CREDITS

President & CEO: TOM WIERZBICKI
Editorial Director: MARY V. GREEN
Managing Editor: TINA COOK
Design Director: STAN GREEN
Developmental Editor: KAREN COSTELLO SOLTYS
Technical Editor: ROBIN STROBEL
Copy Editor: MELISSA BRYAN
Production Manager: REGINA GIRARD
Illustrators: KAY MACKENZIE AND ADRIENNE SMITKE
CD Designer: ADRIENNE SMITKE
Cover & Text Designer: STAN GREEN
Photography: BRENT KANE

Printed in China
16 15 14 13 12 11      8 7 6 5 4 3 2 1

**Library of Congress Cataloging-in-Publication
Data is available upon request.**

ISBN: 978-1-60468-022-5

## MISSION STATEMENT
Dedicated to providing quality products
and service to inspire creativity.

# ACKNOWLEDGMENTS

Thank you, Martingale & Company! *Easy Appliqué Blocks* (2009) was a trip to the candy store for me, and now you're letting me do it again!

Hugs to all of you appliqué enthusiasts who tell me that the CD concept is working for you just as I envisioned: a library of designs right at your fingertips whenever you need one block, or many! It does my heart good to hear from you that my idea works.

My dear husband of more than 20 years, Dana Mackenzie, you understand me so well. We embrace the driven, writerly life together.

My little dog, Willie, is by my side in the studio every day, offering dog help and boon companionship.

All of my friends in the wide world of quilting, whether I've met you yet or not, thank you for your encouragement and validation.

*Kay*

# CONTENTS

# GREETINGS, FELLOW APPLIQUÉ ENTHUSIASTS!

If you're reading this, it's safe to say that you're already a fan of appliqué. Three cheers! Either you're an avid appliquér, you'd like to learn more, or you're eager to get started on this beautiful form of quiltmaking. Welcome, one and all!

## THE BLOCKS

My first book for Martingale & Company, *Easy Appliqué Blocks: 50 Designs in 5 Sizes*, is eclectic in nature, full of fun designs in a variety of styles from offbeat, modern, and whimsical to traditional looking. The traditional blocks attracted me so much that I turned my attention to creating a whole library of them for this new collection.

The blocks in this book recall that old-time vintage flavor and feel, but are simplified for the modern quilter. You'll find baskets and flowers and wreaths and vines, birds and berries and more. This is a whole library of designs that you can reach for any time you want a block (or many), while remembering the appliqué enthusiasts who went before.

## THE METHODS

The world of appliqué offers many different methods, including a myriad of variations within broad categories of technique. There's no right or wrong way. Appliquérs sometimes prefer to stick with what they've learned first. Others gravitate toward a certain method that works for them and gives them satisfying results. What works is not the same for everybody, and all methods are good! This little book provides designs for your appliqué pleasure as you use your favorite methods and your own creative instincts.

Beginning on page 32, you'll find information on my two favorite appliqué methods, one by hand and one by machine. For hand appliqué, there are first some general tips, and then the ingenious back-basting method of preparation. We'll go over what I have to share about hand stitching smooth curves, pointy points, and sharp notches. Following the section on hand appliqué are instructions for raw-edge machine appliqué using paper-backed fusible web.

Whatever your method, pick your favorite designs and stitch them with fun!

# PRINTING BLOCKS FROM THE CD

Modern technology in the form of a CD makes a great partner for this book.

From the companion CD located on the inside back cover, you'll be able to print the blocks you've chosen in five different sizes: 6", 8", 9", 10", or 12". Larger sizes will automatically print out as multiple pages; just trim and tape them together and you'll be ready to go. Reversed versions are also included. Your life just got easier! There's no flipping and tracing, figuring of percentages, or trips to the copy shop.

## WHAT YOU NEED

The CD is designed to work on PC and Mac platforms.

To use the CD you need a CD-ROM drive, a PDF reader, an Internet browser, and a printer. (The browser is the component that runs the CD and allows you to access any of the links provided.) You probably already have the software you need on your computer, but if you have trouble using the CD, you might need to upgrade your software.

The browser runs the CD, whether you're online or not. If you can connect to the Internet, you already have a browser. Some of the really old browsers may have difficulty running the CD. Internet Explorer version 6 and later, Google chrome 7.0 and later, Safari version 3 and later, and Firefox version 2 and later are all compatible. You can upgrade your browser by visiting the provider's website.

The actual patterns are PDF files. Examples of PDF readers are Adobe Reader and, on Mac systems, Apple's Preview. If you don't have a PDF reader installed, you can download Adobe's version free. Just go to: http://www.adobe.com to download and install the reader that's compatible with your operating system.

## HOW IT WORKS

Insert the CD into your CD-ROM drive. Open the CD and click the "Inspired by Tradition" file to open it. Some browsers may display a warning screen about active content. There is no active content on the CD and you can feel safe about disregarding the warning. Click "Enter" to begin.

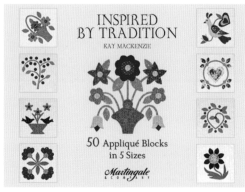

ENTER

Begin by reviewing the copyright information. These are patterns for your own personal use as the owner of *Inspired by Tradition*. It's important to realize that the patterns in electronic form are covered by the same protections as paper patterns. That means, gentle quilter, no printing for a friend, emailing, posting on the Internet, and so on.

The first time you use the CD, it's a good idea to test your printer settings to make sure the blocks are printing at the correct size. Use the navigation bar at the top of the page or the link lower on the page to go to the "Pattern Test" page.

Follow the directions on the "Pattern Test" page to print the test. Some computers think they're being helpful by slightly scaling down files before printing. Unfortunately, there are several places this sizing down can occur. If the size of the printed test pattern is not correct, check your page setup, printer settings, and PDF-reader settings to be certain the documents are set to *print at 100% with no scaling or reduction to fit the page, margins, printable area, etc.*

When you're satisfied that the file is printing correctly, return to the CD and proceed to the "Block Index."

You'll find both an alphabetical listing and thumbnail images of the blocks. Click on your selected block and you'll be taken to its "Block Page."

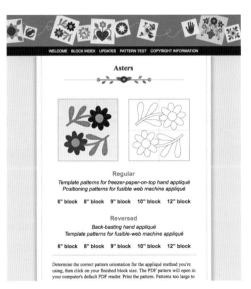

On the "Block Page," determine the correct pattern orientation. Back-basting hand appliqué and fusible machine appliqué both use reversed patterns, but you may be using a different method. Fusible machine appliqué also requires a regular unreversed pattern for placement.

Choose your size. Under the selected orientation, click the finished block size you've chosen. Depending on the individual settings on your computer, the PDF pattern will either download or open. Print your pattern. If the block is larger than will fit on letter-size paper, multiple pages will automatically print. Trim and tape them together for your accurate full-size pattern.

Easy peasy! Once your block has printed, return to the "Block Page." From there you can click back to the "Block Index" and print some more blocks!

The above information also appears on the "Welcome" page so that it'll be handy when you're using the CD. When you're done printing, simply eject the CD at any point. Be sure to put it back in its pocket with the book.

---

## ENLARGING BLOCKS BY PHOTOCOPYING

If you don't have access to a computer and printer, you can enlarge the printed designs in the book using a photocopier. The patterns in the book are printed 3" x 3". To enlarge the printed patterns, photocopy according to the following percentages:

6" block—200%
8" block—266%
9" block—300%

For larger sizes, fold the pattern in halves or quarters, enlarge each section by the same percentage, then trim and tape the sections together.

10" block—333%
12" block—400%

# BLOCK LIBRARY

These classic designs can be used in a multitude of fashions.
Here are just a few ideas to spark your imagination.

WALL QUILTS ☙ APRONS ☙ SMALL QUILTS ☙ SAMPLER QUILTS ☙ VESTS
☙ BED QUILTS ☙ BABY QUILTS ☙ TABLE RUNNERS ☙ LAP QUILTS
☙ NAP QUILTS ☙ BANNERS ☙ TABLE TOPPERS ☙ BED TOPPERS ☙ TOTES
☙ THANK-YOU BLOCKS ☙ FLAGS ☙ EXCHANGE BLOCKS ☙ TEA COZIES ☙ TEA TOWELS
☙ POT HOLDERS ☙ PURSES ☙ POSTCARDS ☙ PLACE MATS ☙ PILLOWS ☙ JACKETS
☙ JUMPERS ☙ SWEATSHIRTS ☙ SKIRTS ☙ MANTEL COVERS ☙ DRESSER RUNNERS
☙ SCARVES ☙ EMBROIDERY PATTERNS ☙ WINDSOCKS ☙ AND MORE

Asters

Basket
of
Flowers

Berry
Vine

Birds
and
Basket

Bluebells

**Budding
Tulips**

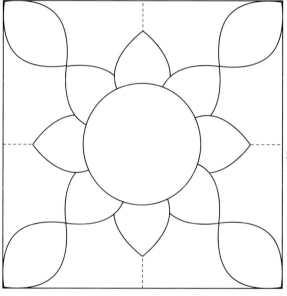

**California
Sunflower**

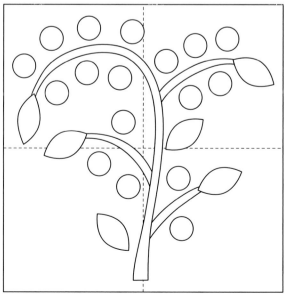

**Cherry
Tree**

**Circle of Hearts**

**Distelfink**

**Dogwood**

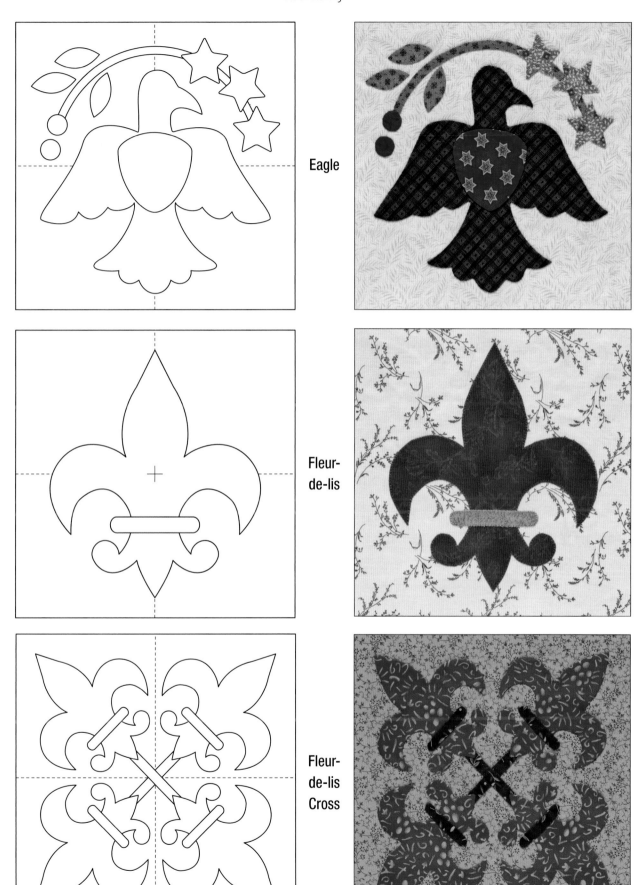

Eagle

Fleur-de-lis

Fleur-de-lis Cross

**Flowering Heart**

**Flowerpot**

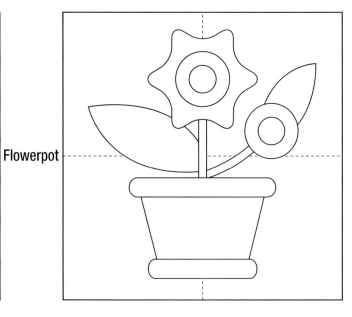

**Forget-me-not**

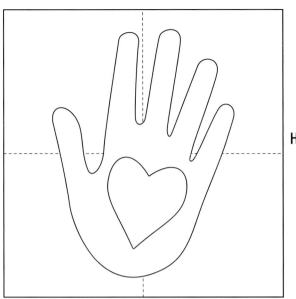

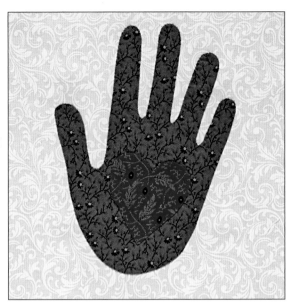

Heart in
Hand

Hearts
and
Petals

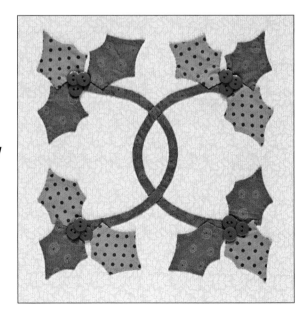

Holly

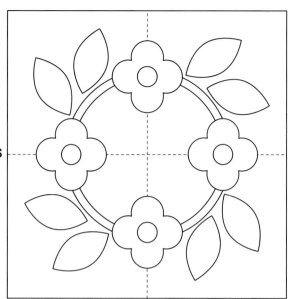

Hollyhocks

Horseshoe
Spray

House-
plant

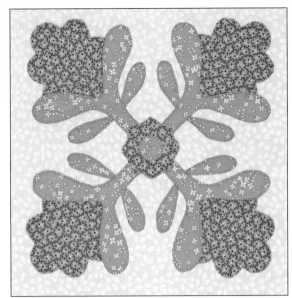

Indiana
Rose

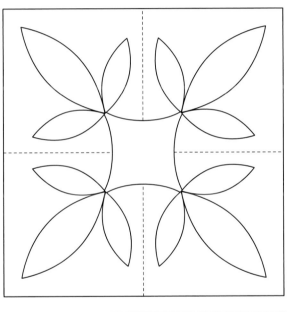

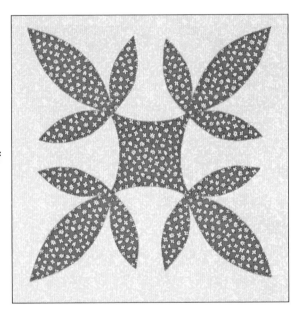

Iris Leaf

Kitten

Laurel
Leaf

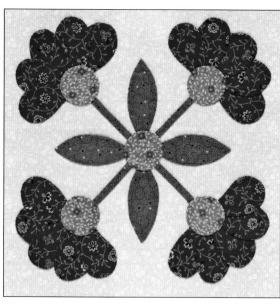

Mexican
Rose

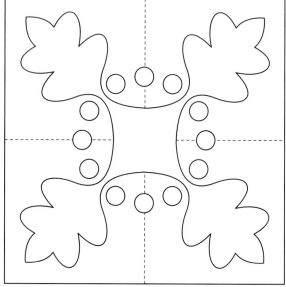

Oak Leaf
and
Cherries

Oak Leaf
and Reel

Ohio
Rose

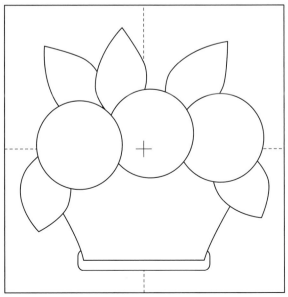

Orange
Basket

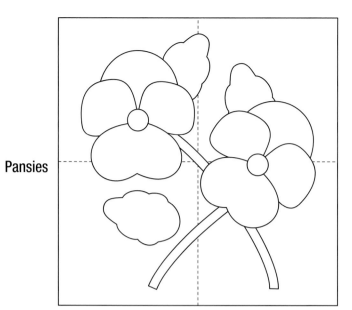

Pansies

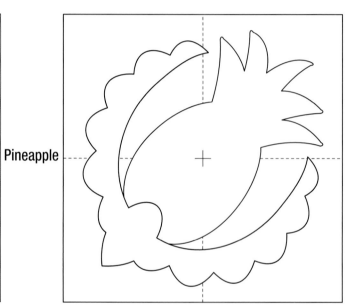

Pineapple

Pome-
granate
and Pink
Buttercup

Prairie
Flower

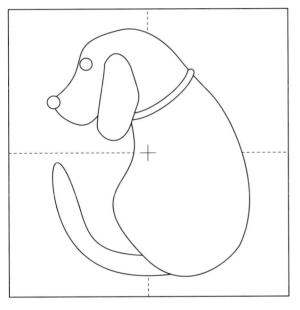

Puppy
Dog

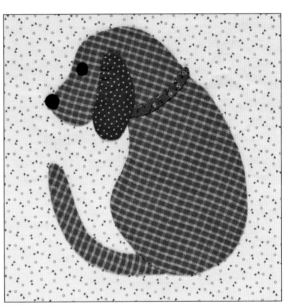

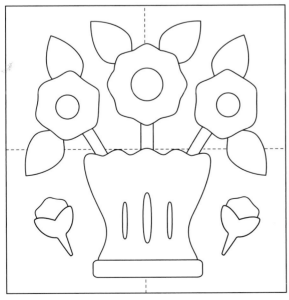

Rose
Basket

Rosebud
Wreath

Snowflake

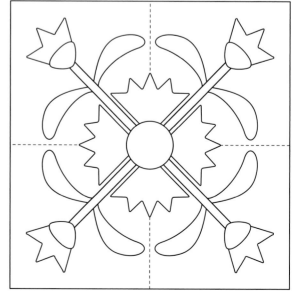

Spice
Pinks

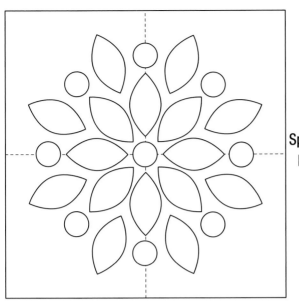

**Spreading Leaves**

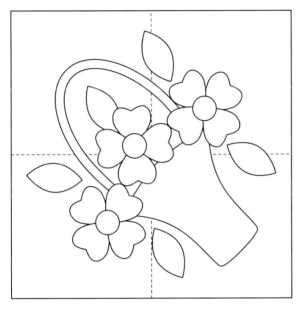

**Spring Basket**

**Three Blooms**

Twirling
Tulips

Urn

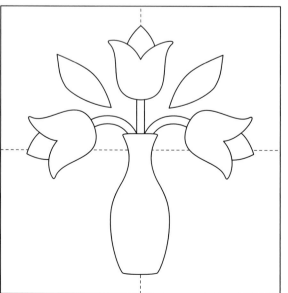

Vase of
Tulips

**Whig Rose**

**Wildflower**

**Wreath of Hearts**

# KAY'S HAND-APPLIQUÉ TIPS

Before we get to the stitching, let's start with some basics.

## FABRIC SELECTION

Choose 100% cotton, medium-weight fabric with a soft, pliable hand. Fabrics containing polyester have "spring" and will resist the creasing needed for needle-turn appliqué. Fabrics that are too thin or loosely woven will ravel easily and wear out more quickly. Fabrics found in independent quilt shops are generally of the highest quality and easiest to work with.

A quick word to the wise: In hand appliqué, prints hide stitches better than solid fabrics. If you'd like to achieve the overall look of solid colors, you can use tone-on-tone prints for added depth and glow. With that said, if you're happy with your hand stitching, don't hesitate to use solids if they give you the look you're after.

## FABRIC PREPARATION

Some quilters prewash their fabrics to remove the sizing, and some prefer to leave the sizing in for added body when piecing. I like the feel of soft, clean fabric, so I'm a washer. I don't think the appliqué

police will come after you if you're not—just make sure to test any suspect fabrics for bleeding issues.

## TOOLS AND NOTIONS

"The right tool for the right job" is an adage that certainly applies to appliqué. Making good selections in the threads, needles, and scissors you use can make a big difference, helping you to avoid frustration and achieve results that please you.

### Scissors

Use sharp, pointy hand scissors, not big shears. My favorite size is 5"; some quilters prefer smaller embroidery scissors. These small scissors give you the control you'll need for precise trimming and clipping.

### Thread

Use fine, thin thread that matches the piece being appliquéd (not the background). I use 50-weight 2-ply cotton machine-embroidery thread. Others use

50-weight 3-ply or 60-weight thread, and still others swear by very fine silk thread. All of these are good choices for hand appliqué. Use what you can find conveniently.

## Needles

Use appliqué needles—yes, even if you have trouble threading them. Size 10 or 11 straw or milliner's needles (they're the same thing) or size 10 or 11 Sharps are excellent choices. Milliner's needles are longer than Sharps, and many appliquérs feel they allow for a better grip. My favorite is a size 10 milliner's needle.

Whatever the number or brand, the important thing is to choose a slender needle that glides through fabric easily without resistance.

## SUGGESTIONS FOR FINE DETAILS

A stem or outline stitch can be used for the whiskers on the kitten. Bring the needle up from the back. Insert it into the background about ⅜" from the start and take a small stitch at 3, coming up halfway between 1 and 2.

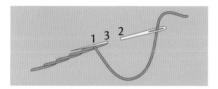

Stem stitch

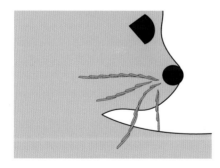

### A THREADING TIP

Instead of holding the needle in midair and trying to poke the thread through the eye, try this method. Cut a fresh end of the thread. Pinch the end between your thumb and forefinger. Slowly open the tips of your thumb and forefinger until the end of the thread is just visible. With the other hand, bring the eye of the needle down over the thread.

Many who swear they cannot thread a needle succeed on the very first try when shown this strategy.

For very small pieces like the eyes and noses of the kitten and puppy, Ultrasuede is one way to go. Ultrasuede is a slightly fluffy synthetic material that doesn't ravel, so you don't have to finish the edges. Look for inexpensive scrap bags of this product to have on hand. Cut the shapes freehand, affix them in place with a tiny amount of fabric-friendly glue, and hand stitch with fine thread, taking small stitches. The thread will sink right into the Ultrasuede and hide from sight. You could use a running stitch close to the edge or a simple whipstitch.

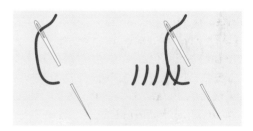

Whipstitch

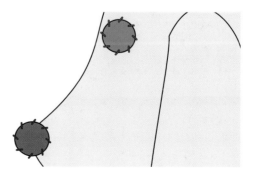

## VISION

If you wear glasses, making sure your prescription is up-to-date is crucial for good appliqué results.

I had 20/20 vision, but at a certain age I had to admit that I found myself with "issues." Does the following sound at all familiar? You can't see the grain of the fabric; you can't see the eye of the needle; you're holding your quilting magazine at arm's length.

Gentle quilter, it's time to go to the drugstore and get some of those groovy granny glasses. Pick up a pill bottle and try on pairs of reading glasses until you can read the teeny-tiny writing on the label.

Presbyopia, otherwise known as "over-40 eyes," is a natural process that causes stiffening in the eye's focusing mechanism, making it difficult to see small things close up. Nonprescription reading glasses magnify the small things and restore details to your vision that you might not have even noticed were missing. This is very important for good appliqué results.

## LIGHTING

Good lighting goes hand in hand with good vision for supporting the success of your appliqué efforts. If your sewing light is just adequate, make a special effort to arrange for more lighting or lighting that is better directed on your work. Overhead lighting, such as a ceiling light, really isn't sufficient for close-up work. Invest in a lamp for your work area that can be directed as needed to illuminate your appliqué.

# BACK-BASTING PREPARATION

How about a method of appliqué that gives super-accurate results, yet uses no glue, no starch, no templates, no freezer paper, no fusible web, no fusible interfacing, no vinyl or tracing paper— just fabric, needle and thread, scissors, and a marking implement. That's my kind of method!

If you like hand appliqué, you might just love back-basting. It's not new, but it may have been flying along under the radar for a lot of appliqué fans. I heard about back basting—aka the no-template method, aka the template-free method—a number of times before I finally wrapped my brain around it. Once I tried it, I was quickly convinced of its benefits, and now I'm a total convert.

Whatever you call this method, there's no faster way to get to the stitching. Cut a background square, select your appliqué fabrics, trace the pattern once, and sew!

The preparation is unusual in this method, but the actual stitching of the motifs is just the same as in traditional hand appliqué. Stitching order is also the same, beginning with pieces that are partially behind other pieces and building to the front. Clipping and stitching of curves, points, and notches—also just the same.

Once you see how it works, put back-basting into your appliqué bag of tricks and use it whenever you like. Start with projects that have bigger pieces and work your way to smaller ones as you become more comfortable with the method.

## OVERVIEW

With this method, your finished appliqué will be a mirror image of the pattern that you trace. Symmetrical patterns do not need to be reversed. To have an asymmetrical pattern appear as it does in the book, print a reversed version from the CD. Larger patterns will print on several pages. Trim and tape the pages together as indicated on the pattern to make the full-size design.

Next, you'll center and trace the entire pattern onto the wrong side of the background fabric. Then, one shape at a time, you'll hold rough-cut appliqué fabrics to the front of the block and baste them to the background fabric from the wrong side along the drawn lines.

On the front, using the basting stitches as a guide, trim the appliqué fabric to the shape of the motif, leaving a turning allowance.

Turn under the edge and stitch the motifs in place, clipping and removing the basting stitches a few at a time. When the stitching is complete, remove the markings from the back of the block.

I have provided step-by-step instructions and a practice piece for you on page 36.

## NOTIONS

Here are the supplies you'll need for the back-basting method.

- A large, thick needle (size 7 or 8) for basting.
- An appliqué needle; use your favorite. (See the information on page 33.)
- Hand-quilting thread, or any thick thread in a bright color for basting.
- Appliqué thread; use your favorite. (See the information on page 32.)
- Sharp, pointy hand scissors.
- Pins.
- Marking implement. I like using a water-erasable marking pen because it's easy to mark with, easy to see, and easily removed. You can also use a marking pencil.
- Light box or light-colored surface.

### WATER-ERASABLE CAUTION

If you're using a water-erasable marking pen, test any suspect appliqué fabrics for colorfastness, because it will be necessary to dampen the block to remove the markings. Follow the manufacturer's instructions for removal.

## PRACTICE PIECE

Here's a full-size 6" x 6" Heart block for you to
practice on. For ease of use, copy or trace this
pattern onto a separate sheet of paper, including the
centering lines at the edges. Then follow the step-by-
step instructions.

# BACK-BASTING STEP BY STEP

At first this method may seem a bit counterintuitive, but follow the steps and soon back-basting will make total sense to you.

1.  Cut an oversize (7" x 7") piece of background fabric. (After the block is completed, you'll trim it to the unfinished size.) Fold in quarters and lightly crease the outer edges to create centering marks. Unfold.
2.  Place the pattern *face up* on a light box or light-colored surface. (This pattern is symmetrical and does not need to be reversed.)
3.  Place the background fabric *face down* on the pattern. Line up the creases with the centering marks on the pattern.
4.  On the wrong side of the fabric, trace the entire pattern. Trace accurately; this is your stitching guide. Do not trace centering lines.

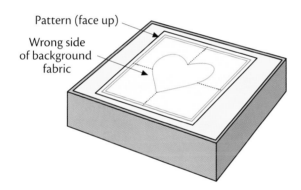

Pattern (face up)

Wrong side of background fabric

5.  Rough cut a piece of appliqué fabric that's larger than your motif–in this case, a heart. Flip the background fabric over so that the right side faces up and place the appliqué fabric, right side up, approximately over the tracing.
6.  Hold both fabrics up to the light, and viewing from the back, position the appliqué fabric so that it completely covers the marked shape, with at least ¼" margin all the way around. Pin.

Position motif fabric on the front
and pin from the back.

7.  Thread the basting needle with thick basting thread that contrasts well with the appliqué. With the wrong side facing you, baste through both layers all the way around the motif with a small running stitch exactly on the drawn line. Leave a short tail at the end. Remove the pins.

Running stitch

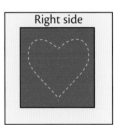

Wrong side

Right side

8.  Turn the project over and, from the right side, trim the appliqué fabric to the shape of the heart, leaving about ³⁄₁₆" outside the basting line.

9.  Clipping and removing a few basting stitches at a time, tuck the turning allowance under and stitch the heart using an appliqué needle and matching thread. For information on smooth curves, sharp notches, and pointy points, see "Hand Stitching" on page 39.

    The appliqué fabric turns easily along the perforations left by the basting thread; the perforations on the background fabric serve as a stitching line. Another benefit of this method is that you can flip the project over from time to time to check your stitch positioning against the markings.

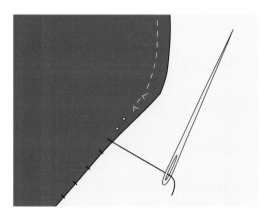

10. Many patterns have pieces that overlap. Use longer basting stitches on areas that will be overlapped by another piece, such as the leaf shown. When trimming the appliqué shape on the front, leave a wider margin in the overlapped area.

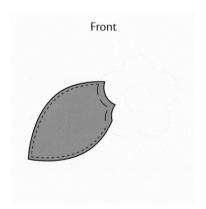

Front

11. Once the shape is appliquéd, remove the long basting stitches and either tie off the appliqué thread or use it to baste the unstitched area to the background. (See "Tying Off the Thread" on page 43.)

### STEMS OR VINES

In back basting, you don't need to take the extra step of making bias tape. You can treat stems and vines like any other shape and they stitch up beautifully, ending up just where they're marked without shifting out of place. Back basting helps you stitch them with smooth, even widths.

Now that you've become acquainted with back-basting, use it some more! As with anything new, success and comfort come with practice.

# HAND STITCHING

Now that your appliqué is all prepped, it's time to stitch! From here on, back basting is the same as traditional needle-turn appliqué, simply removing the basting a little ahead of your stitching.

## CLIPPING

In notches, clip almost to the turn line with the tip of your scissors. Fairly steep inside curves will need a series of shallow clips. Do not clip outer curves.

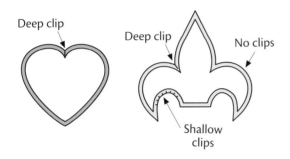

## HOLDING THE PROJECT

When stitching, hold your work from the bottom in your nonsewing hand. This hand should always stay in a neutral position, without bending or twisting the wrist. Fold or roll the project until you can get an over-and-under grip on the section you're working on, just ahead of where you're stitching. Your thumb is on top and your fingers are underneath. They hold the background and the turned edge of the motif just ahead of where you're placing your stitch.

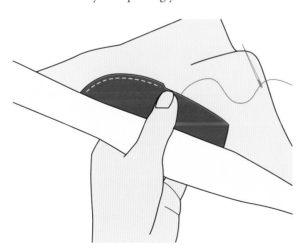

Avoid holding the project in any position where your wrist is twisted or bent.

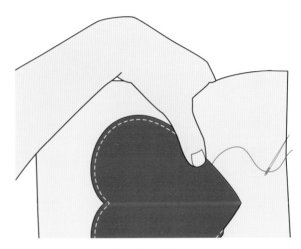

This position is bad for your wrist.

Adjust your grip as often as necessary to get the proper access and angle for stitching. Don't let go with your gripping hand while turning the edge. Use your sewing hand to work with the appliqué pieces.

## SUPPORTING THE PROJECT

Support your work. Holding the project up in midair allows the background fabric to fall away from your hands, which encourages the appliqué to buckle. Put your feet up on a footstool and sew in your lap, not up close to your face. If you need better light or better glasses, I encourage you to seek ways of improving these situations.

The 12" quilter's pressing-and-cutting mat is an excellent appliqué aid. The cushioned side comfortably supports your hand and the project on your lap as you stitch. You can also use a small throw pillow to support your work.

## STITCHING

Load your appliqué needle with the fine thread of your choice. Very long lengths will tangle and become worn, so cut yours about 18" to 20" long and put a small, tight knot in the end.

Choose the area where you'll begin stitching. Motifs that stand alone can be started anywhere, but it's usually best to start on the straightest part. For circles, you can start anywhere! More about circles later.

If part of the motif is overlapped, begin at the point where it first emerges from the upper motif. Right-handed stitchers sew counterclockwise and left-handed sew clockwise. Fold or roll the project and get a good grip on the selected area with your nonsewing hand (keeping your wrist in a neutral position).

Needle-turn appliqué means just that—the turning allowance is turned under with the needle. I call my personal variation "finger pinch, needle poke." While holding the needle temporarily in my curled-up second finger, I use my forefinger and thumb to tuck and pinch the turning allowance under, less than ½" ahead of where I'm stitching.

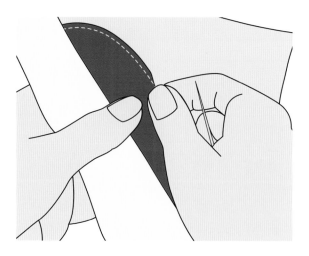

I then use the needle to make small refinements to the stitching edge if needed.

Try using only the needle to turn the fabric and try pinching with the fingers. Use the technique that you're most comfortable with and that gives you results you like.

To begin, create the first ½" of turned-under edge and hold it with your gripping hand. Some appliquérs bring the needle up inside the fold. I

start my thread in the back, bringing my needle up through the background fabric and catching a couple of threads of the fold.

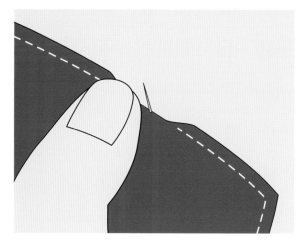

Where do you place your needle for the next stitch? You won't really be able to see it, but visualize going back in exactly where you just came out. Avoiding the motif edge, insert the needle into the background fabric only, just where the last stitch came out.

Push the needle tip forward just slightly, traveling underneath the background fabric. Come back up through the background a very short distance ahead and catch a couple threads of the fold.

Draw up the thread, pulling it out at a right angle to the edge of the motif. Laying the thread out at a right angle helps you gauge exactly where the last stitch came out. Stitches that are placed ahead of or behind this spot will be angled stitches, which are longer and more conspicuous.

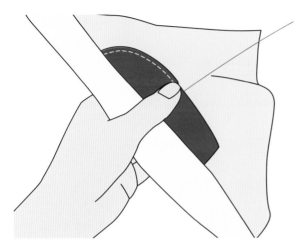

"Sink" your stitches. As you pull up the thread after each stitch, give it a gentle hint of a tug—not so much as to pull up or pucker the piece, but just enough to make the stitch sink into the fold.

Each stitch is taken and placed individually. There is no modern shortcut in hand appliqué. Speed increases with experience and confidence. Also, sew with calm hands. Appliqué should not resemble a wrestling match.

Do not turn or sew sections that will be overlapped by another piece.

### IT'S THE TIP

However you sew, by hand or machine, appliquéing or piecing, remember that it's what the tip of the needle is doing that's important. The rest of the needle just follows.

## SMOOTH CURVES

As you work around a curve, make sure the turning allowance doesn't fold or wrinkle up on itself as you tuck it under. If that happens, you'll get a bump. Don't sew in a bump; it's not going to get better later. Before stitching, take a moment to manipulate the turning allowance underneath the fold with your needle, distributing the bulk and smoothing out the curve.

## POINTS

Stitches are exaggerated for illustration purposes.

1. Sew to within two or three stitches of the point. Trim off the folded-under puppy-dog ear that is sticking out on the other side of the point.

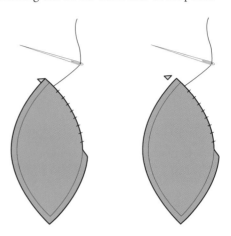

2. Fold the tip under, square across the point.

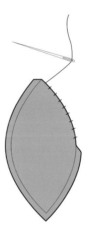

3. Take the remaining stitches to the point, with the last one coming right out of the tip.

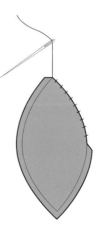

4. Turn the project.

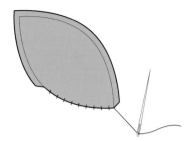

5. Starting at the point, tuck the turning allowance under. Don't try to start ahead and then work back to the point. There will be nowhere for the turning allowance to go. Work from the point forward.

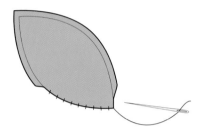

6. When all is arranged satisfactorily and the point looks good, continue to stitch.

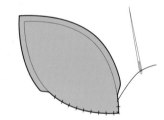

*Leaves are a common motif in appliqué, and they offer a great opportunity to practice your points.*

## NOTCHES

1. Clip the notch almost to the turn line.

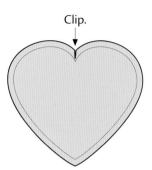

2. Sew to within two or three stitches of the notch. There will be very little turning allowance in this area. That's okay. Use very small stitches and tuck under any loose threads.

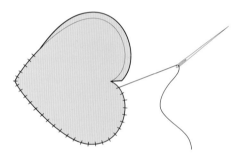

3. Turn the project. Tuck under the first bit of turning allowance on the other side of the notch. In this illustration, some ornery threads from the motif fabric are sticking up in the notch. The needle is not stitching; it's behind the motif, ready to sweep the loose threads under.

4. Use the shaft of the needle to sweep across the notch, creating a tiny fold and encouraging any loose threads to go under. As mentioned before, the needle still is not stitching, just sweeping.

5. Take the remaining stitches to the notch. The last one, directly in the notch, should pick up three or four threads of the motif fabric.

6. Sweep again if necessary. With the tip of the needle, dig under the motif fabric and insert the needle into the background exactly where the last stitch came out. Swing the needle and come out going forward for the next stitch. Snug the thread down well to create a sharp notch.

*A heart is a classic motif for learning how to handle both points and notches.*

## TYING OFF THE THREAD

On the final stitch, insert the needle through the background and pull it all the way through to the back. Turn the block over. Right next to the thread, take a tiny tack in the background fabric beneath the motif and slowly pull the loop down. Before the loop is closed, put the needle through it, and then snug the loop down. (Make another tack if you like, but I decided a while ago that I would save days and years of my life by doing only one.) Bury the thread tail by running the needle between the background and the motif before cutting it off.

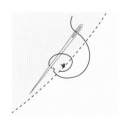

If a raw edge to be left unsewn is of any size, you can run your thread behind the background up into the unsewn margin and baste across it. In this case, I skip the tying-off process and finish with a backstitch. The motif isn't going anywhere, because it will be stitched over by another piece.

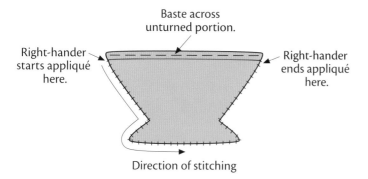

Remove the large back-basting stitches across the unsewn margin as you complete each piece.

## CIRCLES

There are several tools on the market to help make nice circles. Check the gadget section of your favorite quilt shop. A simple low-tech way to make a prepared-edge circle is to use a running stitch to gather the circle around a cardboard or plastic template and then press a crease into it.

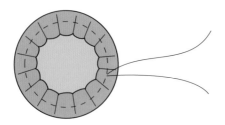

Personally, I appliqué circles just like any other shape. For marking, I use a circle template tool that I got at an art-supply store, choosing a size that is a little bit bigger than the circle on the pattern. (When you trace, the circle shrinks.) Back-basting with a well-drawn circle gives a precise stitching guide on the back to help make the circles pleasingly round.

If the last little bit of turning allowance is trying to form itself into a bump as it goes under, I use my needle to do some back-and-forth adjustment under the fold to distribute the bulk.

Circles can also be buttons, or yo-yos! Consider these for berries or cute flower centers. See the Holly block on page 21.

*Try different methods for making nice, round circles such as these three on the Rose Basket block (page 27)*

## MORE CONTRAST

You can outline the edges of your motifs to make them stand out more from the background fabric. If working by hand, use embroidery floss and a simple backstitch to delineate the edges.

Backstitch

## THE FINAL TRIM

When all pieces are stitched, lay the block face down on a fluffy towel and remove any water-erasable markings according to the manufacturer's instructions. Allow to air dry, and then press the block.

After pressing, trim the block to its unfinished size. Now start another, fellow appliqué enthusiast!

*The light pink fabric chosen for the dogwood doesn't show up well against the cream background.*

*A little hand embroidery around the edges helps a lot.*

# RAW-EDGE MACHINE APPLIQUÉ

You can show off your thread collection and save some time in the stitching too with this popular appliqué method.

## MATERIALS

Here's what you'll need before you get started.

- Fabrics: Prewash your appliqué fabrics. The sizing in unwashed fabric may interfere with the bond of the fusible web.

   For raw-edge appliqué, it's best to choose fabrics where the main color goes all the way through. Whitish or sketchy-looking backs may show along the edges of the cut motifs. If there's such a fabric you really want to use, stitch a test and try touching up any pale edges with a matching permanent fabric marker.
- Sewing machine with either a blanket stitch or an adjustable zigzag stitch.
- Open-toed presser foot.
- Sharp machine needle in a small size, such as 70/10.
- Lightweight or regular-weight paper-backed fusible web.
- Thread: I use a fine thread, usually 50-weight 2-ply cotton thread, in a matching color to give a softer, less obvious look. Use a contrasting color or a heavier thread and a larger needle if you prefer a more defined look for the edges of your appliqués. The combination of black thread and a larger blanket stitch mimics old-fashioned handwork.
- Scissors that you don't mind using to cut paper
- Light box may be needed.
- Tracing paper may be needed.
- Tear-away or wash-away stabilizer may be needed.

## PATTERN PREPARATION

With this method, your finished appliqué will be a mirror image of the pattern that you use for making templates. Symmetrical patterns do not need to be reversed. To have an asymmetrical pattern appear as it does in the book, print a *reversed* version from the CD. This will be your *template pattern*. Write "Template" on the pattern. (Larger patterns will print on several pages. Trim and tape the pages together as indicated on the pattern to make the full-size design.)

   Print an additional *unreversed* pattern. This will be your *positioning pattern*. Label it "Positioning."

## TEMPLATE PREPARATION

Each motif needs its own template. Using the *template pattern*, trace each appliqué piece individually onto the paper side of the fusible web, leaving at least ½" between pieces. A pencil is fine for this. To indicate a portion of a piece that is overlapped by another piece, use a dashed line.

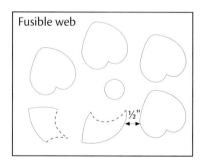

Fusible web

Cut out each template roughly, about ¼" outside the lines.

To reduce stiffness in the finished quilt, remove the center portion of all but the smallest templates. Cut through the edge of each template to about ¼" inside the drawn line and trim away the center, leaving a ring of paper-backed fusible web in the shape of the motif.

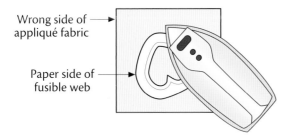

## MOTIF PREPARATION

Using a dry iron and following the manufacturer's recommendations, press the templates *fusible side down* onto the *wrong* side of the appliqué fabrics.

Wrong side of appliqué fabric

Paper side of fusible web

Allow fabric and templates to cool briefly. Handling as little as possible, cut the motif area apart from the main body of the fabric, and then roughly cut the motifs apart.

The next step is to carefully cut out the motifs exactly on the *solid* pencil lines. Leave a little fabric outside *dashed* lines.

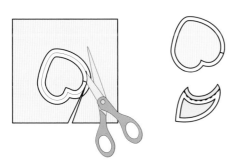

## STEMS OR VINES

You can use bias tape for stems or vines, or you can fuse them like any other shape.

To make bias strips, I reach for my trusty gadget—the ¼" or ⅜" bias-tape maker. This tool automatically folds the edges of the fabric to make bias tape of a nice even width. Bias-tape makers come in progressively wider sizes. Just be aware that the wider the bias strip, the less likely it is to go around a tight curve smoothly. Wider stems are probably easier to handle by fusing.

Here's how I get the bias-tape maker to work easily for me.

1. For the ¼"-wide gadget, cut a ⅝"-wide strip of fabric on the bias. For the ⅜"-wide gadget, cut the bias strip ⅞" wide. Trim the top of the strip at an angle upward to the left. (It seems to feed through the gadget better this way.)

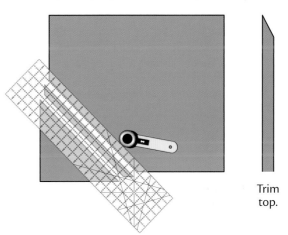

Trim top.

For straight stems, cut the strips on the straight grain instead of on the bias. They wiggle less.

2. Poke the point at the end of the strip right side up into the gadget until you can see the fabric in the slot on top. Use the tip of a pin to pull the strip along the slot until it sticks out the narrow end. Pin this folded end of the strip to the ironing board. Be sure to use a glass-head pin so you don't have to worry about melting a plastic pin.

3. Using a hot iron and plenty of steam, pull the gadget along the strip with one smooth, fairly rapid motion, following it closely with the iron. *Hold your iron so that the steam vents are not*

*directed at your fingers.* Don't stop partway through or try to back up. Pulling smoothly is important for getting nicely formed bias tape.

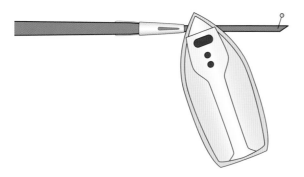

## BACKGROUND FABRIC PREPARATION

Cut the background square a little larger than the unfinished size. For an 8" block (8½" unfinished), cut the background at least 9" square. After the block is completed, you'll trim it to the unfinished size.

Fold the background square in quarters and crease the outer edges to create centering marks. Unfold the square.

If using bias tape for stems and vines, place the *positioning pattern* underneath the background fabric and trace each stem, strip, or vine on the *right* side of the fabric with one central line, plus a beginning and ending mark. A light pencil mark will suffice. For example, for this pattern, mark the background square this way.

## MAKING BIAS STRIPS FUSIBLE

You can make bias or straight strips fusible by applying thin strips of paper-backed fusible web. The product comes on a roll and can be found alongside the bias-tape makers in the notions section of your favorite quilt shop.

I apply the fusible web with a dry iron as a separate step, right after making the bias tape. I prefer to cut the web in half lengthwise so that there is only a tiny amount applied in the center on the wrong side of the bias tape. This will be enough to keep the stems or vines secure for stitching.

## POSITIONING MOTIFS

Putting the pieces where they're supposed to go is easy and accurate using a combination of direct marking for bias-tape stems (see previous section) and the *positioning pattern* or an *overlay* for everything else.

### Stems or Vines

It depends on the pattern, but stems or vines are often the first elements to go down.

If using bias tape, position the prepared strips along the previously marked lines on the background fabric. Trim to the proper length, leaving a generous extra amount on either end. You can easily trim off what you don't need later.

Remove the paper backing from the fusible web and fuse the strips in place with a hot steam iron, molding the strips along curves.

If you haven't used fusible web, there are a couple of other ways to hold the strips in place. I've found that a little glue can be my friend. A dab of glue stick works fine to secure these elements in place for stitching. Or, you can thread baste them in place.

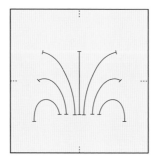

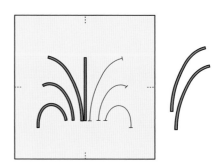

## Other Motifs

Place your *positioning pattern* on a light-colored surface (for instance, another piece of white paper), put the background fabric *right side up* over it (lined up with centering marks), remove the paper backing from the motifs, and position all the pieces for the block at once. Carefully transfer to the ironing board for fusing.

If you can't see the pattern clearly enough, add a light box underneath.

If the background fabric is still too dark to see through, trace the *positioning pattern* onto tracing paper, including the centering marks. Place this overlay on top of the background fabric and line it up with the creases. Position the motifs under the tracing-paper overlay.

## FUSING

On the ironing board, remove the positioning pattern or overlay. Following the manufacturer's recommendations, steam press the appliqué pieces until they're bonded to the background. Don't move the iron back and forth across the motifs, just pick the iron up and set it down until all sections are fused. Let cool, and then move to the sewing machine.

## SEWING

Start by testing your stitching on a scrap project. Using a blanket stitch or a narrow zigzag and the thread of your choice, experiment with stitch length and width until you're satisfied with the tension and the appearance of the stitching.

For blanket stitching, the length of the forward stitch and the sideways stitch should be the same. The forward stitches go into the background fabric, right next to the motif. The sideways stitches bite into the motif at a right angle to the edge.

If you have any trouble with "tunneling" (stitching that puckers the project), use tear-away stabilizer underneath your project and remove it once you're finished sewing.

Start stitching just where a motif emerges from underneath another one, and end where it goes back under. Sew slowly and steer around curves as much as you can. When you need to pivot, stop with the needle down in the background fabric. Raise the presser foot, pivot the project, lower the presser foot, and continue sewing. Around tight curves, it's better to make frequent small pivots than fewer large ones.

Use strategic pivoting to keep the sideways stitches biting into the motif at a right angle, including points and notches.

I'm fond of matching the thread to the motif. If you do this too, sew all areas of one color—such as all the pink—before changing threads and moving on to the next color.

*This motif fabric with lots of white doesn't contrast much with the light background.*

*A dark thread used for the blanket stitch defines the edge.*

Draw the bobbin thread up to the top when beginning your line of stitching, and leave a length of thread tails. When you've finished that line of stitching, leave a thread tail as well. Load the thread tails onto a large-eyed needle and pull them through to the back, burying them in the line of stitching before cutting them off.

To help low-contrast motifs stand out more from the background, choose a contrasting thread or a darker color in the same family.

You can topstitch bias stems down either side using a straight stitch, or you can use the stitch that matches your other motifs. It's your choice!

After the appliqué is complete, press and trim the block to the unfinished size.

That's machine appliqué—another one for your appliqué bag of tricks!

# FUSIBLE-WEB MANAGEMENT

If you've ever had a tussle with paper-backed fusible web, you might find these few tips useful in keeping the product under control as you work on your machine-appliqué projects.

There are many brands, weights, and styles of fusible web on the shelves of our quilt shops today. The kind we're using in this style of appliqué is lightweight, paper-backed, and comes on a bolt.

TIP 1: First of all, ask the clerk in the store to fold your piece loosely for you instead of rolling it. You know what happens if, say, you place one towel on top of another and roll them up together? The top one scootches along and ends up sticking out farther than the bottom one by the time you're done. I don't know which law of physics makes this so, but the same thing can happen with fusible web and its paper backing.

TIP 2: As soon as you get home, cut the product into squares so it can lie flat. I keep a separate rotary cutter for cutting paper and for this purpose. The width of the product is often 17", so you can cut it into 8½" squares and they'll fit perfectly into a gallon-size ziplock bag.

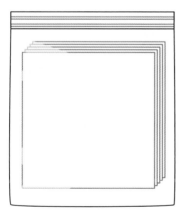

Not only are the squares flat and happy and much easier to work with than a big floppy hunk, but keeping them in a bag protects the product from either drying out or being exposed to humidity.

I keep scraps of fusible web in an old box lid that fits into the zippy bag when not in use.

TIP 3: As I work on a pattern, I start with the smaller pieces of fusible web and only start a new square when there's a motif that's bigger than my biggest scrap. It's so nice to reach into that bag and pull out a fresh, flat sheet in such a manageable size.

TIP 4: Start with a sharp pencil and keep it sharpened as you trace the templates.

**TIP 5:** You can trace the smaller pieces inside the larger pieces. The centers of the fusible-web templates will be cut out to reduce stiffness in the quilt, and using the cut-out area to make another template can save product too.

Let's say we're starting with a pattern like this.

The leaves will fit inside the heart with enough room to spare to cut everything out roughly.

While you're at it, go ahead and trace the flower center inside the flower. Use a circle template tool (see page 44) for well-drawn circles.

**TIP 6:** The smallest, itty-bitty pieces like flower centers are too small to cut out the center. Without that open area it can be hard to get the paper backing started to peel it off when you're ready to fuse. My new favorite strategy is that, once the small motif is fused and rough-cut, I peel up one side of the paper, going into the motif area a little bit.

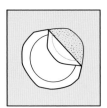

Then I lay the paper back down and cut out the motif on the drawn line. When I'm ready to take the paper off, part of it has already been started.

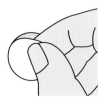

**TIP 7:** To avoid shadow through when using white or very light fabrics over darker fabrics, use a double layer to create the motif.

First fuse two layers of fabric together. Then, use this composed fabric just like the other appliqué fabrics in your project.

# APPLIQUÉ QUESTIONS AND ANSWERS

When I'm chatting with fellow quilters about appliqué, the same questions and concerns come up with regularity. I thought you'd like to hear how I respond to these common appliqué conundrums.

**Q:** What kind of appliqué do I need to use for your patterns?

**A:** Any kind you like; it's all good! There are so many ways to go about it. Appliqué enthusiasts should use the method that suits them best. That's not the same for everybody.

**Q:** I haven't appliquéd before. Which method would you recommend trying first?

**A:** It depends on your nature as an individual. Some quilters prefer hand work, others sew by machine exclusively. Some will only consider turned edges, while others enjoy raw-edge appliqué. Some are drawn to a primitive, rustic effect, and others go for a more refined look. Some would rather spend time on prep work, others want to get straight to the stitching (I'm in that camp). I'd say, learn as much as you can about appliqué and find the method that's just right for you. In this book you'll find instructions for two very different forms of appliqué that will give you a great foundation.

**Q:** I just don't have the patience.

**A:** I always say, it doesn't take patience when you're doing something you enjoy. For me, it takes patience to get the dishes washed, or to get all those other chores out of the way so that I can get to the stitching! If you're not enjoying your appliqué, maybe you just haven't found the method that's right for you.

**Q:** What kind of appliqué do you do?

**A:** My very favorite is back-basting hand appliqué. I also do a fair amount of raw-edge fusible machine appliqué. I like that too, and it does get the job done a little faster.

**Q:** But is *fusible* appliqué "real" appliqué?

**A:** Yes. Yes it is. If you prefer fusible appliqué, hold your head up high and say, "I fuse and I'm proud."

**Q:** Your stitching is so precise. I could never do that.

**A:** Please! I totally believe in do-overs.

In back-basting hand appliqué, there's a built-in stitching guide on the back of the fabric, so it's easy to tell if I'm getting a little off. If I'm veering, I can take out some stitches and do them over.

Also, sometimes when I'm hand stitching a motif and I get back around to the beginning, my beginning and ending stitches aren't aligned with one another. When this happens, I look at both sets of stitches to figure out which one is better aligned with the pattern. If the ending stitches have veered, I take a do-over. If the beginning stitches are not quite spot-on, I clip off the initial knot, release a few stitches, and sew over the gap until everything averages out. I call this "the band-aid maneuver."

Machine appliqué stitches are not as easy to take out, but it can be done if you're just not happy with them. Use a "stitch reversal unit" (aka seam ripper) and be gentle with the stitches and the fabric so that you don't chew up the edge of the appliqué.

In machine appliqué, sometimes my coordination gets off and the machine takes a wild stitch out into the hinterlands. If this happens, I stop, take out the bad stitch, and fasten off the threads before starting again. See "Sewing" on page 49.

**Q:** In hand appliqué I have trouble getting the curves to be smooth.

**A:** The turning allowance is the culprit. It's not distributed evenly underneath the stitched edge. See the information on page 41 about stitching smooth curves. If you've stitched your whole piece and then notice a bump in a curve that should be smooth, try sticking the tip of your needle underneath the turned edge and moving the turning allowance back and forth to distribute the bulk. If that's not going to work, remove a few stitches, adjust the turning allowance, and stitch again, sewing over a few stitches before and a few stitches after the gap, in a band-aid maneuver.

If you've finished a small circle and notice that there are little dimples, you can actually go around again with another round of stitching, placing your stitches strategically to pull in the tiny bumps and smooth out the curve.

**Q:** I just cannot do points.
**A:** Sometimes appliqué instructions tell you to leave ¼" for turning allowance. That's really too much, and creates way too much bulk to stuff under at the point. Trim to about ³⁄₁₆", and be sure to trim off the little ear that sticks out before turning the tip under. (See "Points" on page 41.) A combination of reducing bulk and knowing the steps involved in stitching a point should help.

**Q:** Notches are a problem for me. They always fray.
**A:** It's the nature of the beast that there's little or no turning allowance once you're down into the notch. Don't panic, don't overwork the fabric, and use tiny stitches to corral loose threads and secure the edges of the appliqué in this area. See page 42 for more notch strategies.

**Q:** What is reverse appliqué?
**A:** Appliqué (sometimes referred to as direct appliqué) is covering up the background fabric with a motif. Reverse appliqué is cutting away part of the motif to reveal the background fabric (or another fabric).

There's a touch of reverse appliqué in the Rose Basket block (page 27).

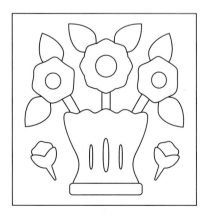

The cutouts in the body of the basket could reveal the background fabric. However, I chose to insert a contrasting fabric. Before basting the basket, place a rough-cut piece of the contrasting fabric on the front of the background fabric, covering the cutout markings, and secure it with large basting stitches.

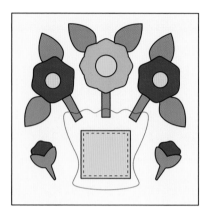

Back baste and trim the basket. Slit the cutouts, being careful not to cut through the contrasting fabric underneath. When the cutouts are stitched, the contrasting fabric will be revealed. Remove the large basting stitches.

**Q:** My fabric shreds along the edges as I machine appliqué. Help!
**A:** Some fabrics just do that more than others. It's prudent to test fabrics that you want to use for raw-edge appliqué, and make sure you're not splintering the edge of the motif with the needle as you sew. If you're already committed to a fabric that's prone to shredding, get out your sharp hand scissors and give the motif a haircut after you're finished stitching.

# A LITTLE GALLERY OF IDEAS

The blocks in this collection are reminiscent of earlier times, with red and green on white and a touch of gold as the appliquér's palette. The designs look beautiful stitched up in those classic colors, but they can also look modern, fresh, and fun with today's updated fabric choices.

Choose your favorite blocks and put them together into a beautiful wall piece, or sprinkle them into sampler quilts. Choose as many or as few as you need for your project—the designs will always be right at your fingertips when you want them.

The Gallery on the following pages presents some examples for your inspiration. The Martingale & Company staff and I had so much fun creating these simple wall quilts, both on the computer and with fabric. We've provided information about the block sizes, sashing, and border dimensions in case you'd like to make something similar. All measurements are given as finished sizes.

Enjoy the blocks!

# COMING UP ROSES

Finished size: 26" x 26"

Prairie Flower, Urn, Rosebud Wreath, and Whig Rose 9" blocks, set with a ½"-wide inner border
and a 3½"-wide outer border. The Rosebud Wreath and outer border are embellished with motifs
taken from the other blocks.

# APPLIQUÉR AT HEART

Finished size: 22" x 46"

The choice of fabrics can create the look and feel you like. Distelfink, Wreath of Hearts , and Flowering Heart blocks sized at 12" are framed with a 1½"-wide checkerboard inner border and a 3½"-wide outer border in this Country French heart-themed banner.

# CHERRY JUBILEE

Finished sizes: 8" x 8"

This charming vignette features three 8" mini quilts with an Americana feel made from
Cherry Tree, Eagle, and Oak Leaf and Cherries blocks.

# SPRING BASKETS

Finished size: 29" x 29"

Four 9" Spring Basket blocks are set with 1"-wide sashing, a 1½-wide inner border,

and a 2½"-wide outer border for a cheerful blooming wall quilt.

# WANNA PLAY?

Finished size: 22" x 13"

Kitten and Puppy Dog blocks, each 9", play on an 18" x 9" background with a 2"-wide border.

# TULIP FESTIVAL TABLE RUNNER

Finished size: 40" x 16"

Two 6" Vase of Tulips blocks equal the height of a 9" Twirling Tulip block when 1½"-wide top and bottom strips are added. The runner is finished with a 2"-wide border.

# BIBLIOGRAPHY

Brackman, Barbara. *Encyclopedia of Appliqué*. Lafayette, California: C&T Publishing, 2009.

Hall, Carrie A., and Rose G. Kretsinger. *The Romance of the Patchwork Quilt in America*. New York, New York: Bonanza Books, 1935.

Havig, Bettina. *Carrie Hall Blocks*. Paducah, Kentucky: American Quilter's Society, 1999.

Joyce, Henry. *Art of the Needle: 100 Masterpiece Quilts from the Shelburne Museum*. Shelburne, Vermont: Shelburne Museum, 2008.

Kimball, Jeana. *Red and Green: An Appliqué Tradition*. Bothell, Washington: That Patchwork Place, 1990.